S0-CFU-165

**Put Beginning Readers on the Right Track with
ALL ABOARD READING™**

The All Aboard Reading series is especially designed for beginning readers. Written by noted authors and illustrated in full color, these are books that children really want to read—books to excite their imagination, expand their interests, make them laugh, and support their feelings. With fiction and nonfiction stories that are high interest and curriculum-related, All Aboard Reading books offer something for every young reader. And with four different reading levels, the All Aboard Reading series lets you choose which books are most appropriate for your children and their growing abilities.

Picture Readers
Picture Readers have super-simple texts, with many nouns appearing as rebus pictures. At the end of each book are 24 flash cards—on one side is a rebus picture; on the other side is the written-out word.

Station Stop 1
Station Stop 1 books are best for children who have just begun to read. Simple words and big type make these early reading experiences more comfortable. Picture clues help children to figure out the words on the page. Lots of repetition throughout the text helps children to predict the next word or phrase—an essential step in developing word recognition.

Station Stop 2
Station Stop 2 books are written specifically for children who are reading with help. Short sentences make it easier for early readers to understand what they are reading. Simple plots and simple dialogue help children with reading comprehension.

Station Stop 3
Station Stop 3 books are perfect for children who are reading alone. With longer text and harder words, these books appeal to children who have mastered basic reading skills. More complex stories captivate children who are ready for more challenging books.

In addition to All Aboard Reading books, look for All Aboard Math Readers™ (fiction stories that teach math concepts children are learning in school) and All Aboard Science Readers™ (nonfiction books that explore the most fascinating science topics in age-appropriate language).

All Aboard for happy reading!

To Izzy—A.S.

To Mom, Dad, Patricia,
Adrian (the younger), and Dorothy
"You can never have too many books"—A.C.S.

Library of Congress Cataloging-in-Publication Data

Schreiber, Anne.
    Magnets / by Anne Schreiber ; illustrated by Adrian C. Sinnott.
    p. cm. — (All aboard science reader. Station stop 3)
    Summary: Introduces different kinds of magnets, hwo they work, and some of the ways in which they are used.
    1. Magnetism—Juvenile literature. [1. Magnetism.] I. Sinnott, Adrian C., ill.
II. Title. III. Series.
QC753.7.S37 2003
538'.4—dc21
                                        2003005233

ISBN 0-448-43149-1 (pbk)   A   B   C   D   E   F   G   H   I   J

ISBN 0-448-43238-2 (GB)   A   B   C   D   E   F   G   H   I   J

MAGNETS

By Anne Schreiber
Illustrated by Adrian C. Sinnott

Grosset & Dunlap • New York

What's strong enough to smash atoms?
What's able to power high-speed trains?
What can fight the force of gravity?
It's in metals. It's in the earth.
It's magnetism!

The Force Is with Us

More than two thousand years ago, in Turkey, a shepherd named Magnes was walking through the mountains near his home. Suddenly, some metal in Magnes's sandal stuck to a rock in the mountain. Was it magic? No, it was magnetism!

Magnes ran back to town with the rock. People came from all around to study it. Today, scientists call the rock magnetite after Magnes. They know that it contains a lot of iron. Iron is a very magnetic kind of metal. That is why the rock acted as a magnet and attracted Magnes's shoe.

Magnetism is an invisible force. Some types of metals have this magnetic force. A material that has a magnetic force is called a magnet.

Today, magnets are everywhere. You probably can't even see some of them. Many will be hidden. But magnets work for you even when you can't see them. Some examples of common everyday magnets are: refrigerator magnets, doorbells, and compasses.

Count the magnets around you right now. How many do you see?

What can a magnet do? It can attract, or pull in, objects made of certain kinds of metals. A magnet can also repel, or push away, other magnets.

Only certain kinds of materials are attracted to magnets. They are iron, steel, cobalt, and nickel. A material that is attracted to magnets is called "magnetic."

Try It

Find out which everyday objects are magnetic.
Collect things from around your house. Make
a prediction: Which objects do you think
will be attracted to the magnet? Now
test your prediction by holding
each object near a magnet. If the
object sticks to the magnet, it's
magnetic. If it does not stick,
it is nonmagnetic.

Write down
your results.

MAGNETIC QUIZ

**If nickel is a magnetic metal, why aren't
nickel coins attracted to magnets?**

Nickels contain only a small amount
of nickel. They're actually
made mostly of copper,
a nonmagnetic metal.

Some magnets are made naturally. Iron, cobalt, and magnetic rock such as magnetite are natural magnets.

Other magnets are human-made. Magnets form when a magnetic material, such as iron or cobalt, is mixed with other metals such as aluminum or copper. Then the magnet is formed into a shape.

Magnets come in all different sizes, shapes, and strengths. Different magnets can do different things, depending on their shapes and sizes. Bar magnets are rectangular and flat. They can do things like hold alphabet letters to the refrigerator. Horseshoe magnets are *U* shaped. They can lift heavy things.

MAGNETITE

IRON

COBALT

BAR
MAGNET

HORSESHOE
MAGNET

Every magnet has two poles. The poles are the points where the magnetic force is the strongest. One pole on a magnet is called the north pole. The other pole is called the south pole.

Try It

Hang a bar magnet from a string. Hold the north pole of a second magnet close by. The south pole of the first magnet will be drawn to it. What do you think will happen if you hold up the south pole of the second magnet? Try it. What happens?

Poles that are the same push each other away, or repel each other. The north pole of one magnet will repel the north pole of another magnet.

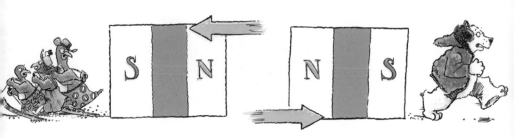

Poles that are opposite pull together, or attract each other. The north pole of one magnet will attract the south pole of another magnet.

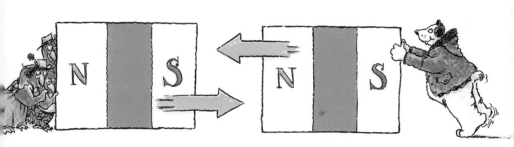

Every magnet has a magnetic field. The magnetic field is the area around the magnet where there is a magnetic force.

The magnetic field begins at each pole and wraps around the magnet. It is an invisible force. You can't see a magnetic field, but you can see how it works.

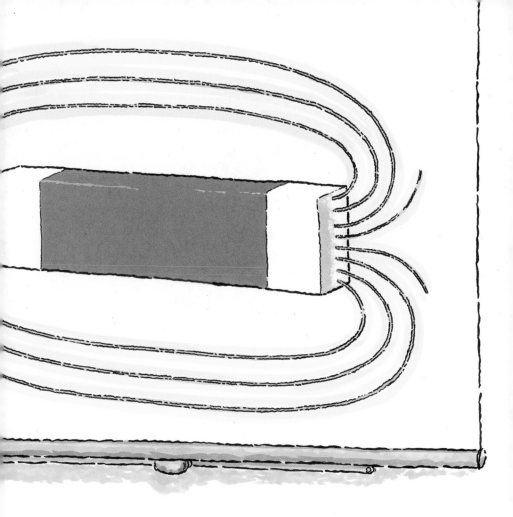

The closer an object is to a magnet, the stronger the magnetic force is on that object. If you move the object away from the magnet, the magnetic force on the object gets weaker.

Why are some materials magnetic
and others nonmagnetic? The answer
is in the small parts that make up
the inside of the magnet.

A bar magnet is made up of lots of little
tiny bar magnets. These tiny parts are
called magnetic domains. Magnetic
domains exist only in a few special kinds

of metals such as iron, nickel, and cobalt. Other metals, like copper or aluminum, don't have magnetic domains.

Just like the magnet itself, each tiny domain has a north pole and a south pole.

If you break a bar magnet in half, you will find that each half will have a north pole and a south pole. If you break it in half again, each new piece will still have a north pole and a south pole. That's because every magnetic domain has exactly two poles.

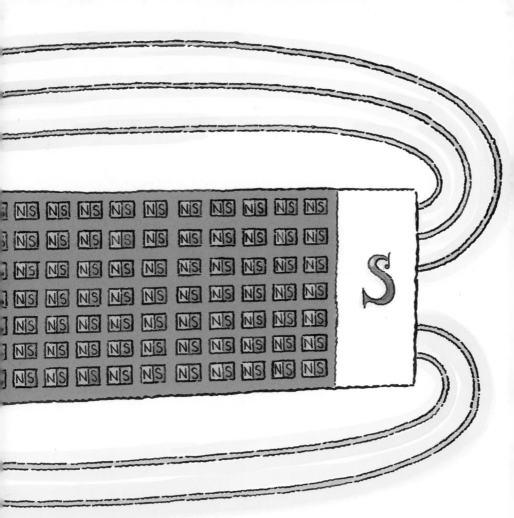

In a bar magnet, the domains are neatly lined up so all the north poles point one way and all the south poles point the other. When all the north poles face the same direction, their individual forces add up. When all the individual forces add up, the metal has a strong magnetic force.

   If metals, such as iron, have magnetic
domains, is a regular iron nail a magnet?
It can be.

   An iron nail is also made up of magnetic
domains. But a nail's domains are not
neatly lined up. Some north poles face
one way, some face another. Because these
poles are not lined up, their forces do not
add up. The nail does not have a strong
north pole or south pole.

A regular iron nail can easily be made into a magnet. All you have to do is line up the magnetic domains. Here's how: When the iron nail is near a magnet, the domains in the nail get turned around to match the magnet's poles. When you take the nail away from the magnet, the domains go back to the way they were.

If you leave the nail near the magnet for long enough, the domains will stay lined up with the magnet. The poles of the iron nail's domains are strong enough to attract other magnetic objects. The iron nail is now a magnet.

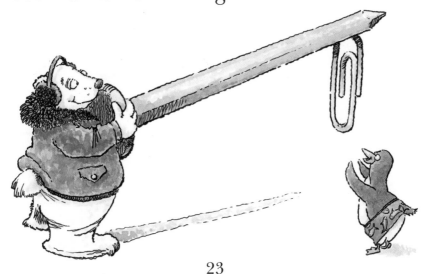

23

Try It

First make sure your nail is really made of a metal that has tiny magnetic domains. If it sticks to the magnet, then it has magnetic domains, and it must be the right kind of metal.

Next, test your nail to make sure it's not already a magnet. Hold the nail near a paper clip. Does the nail attract the paper clip? If not, the nail is not a magnet. Not yet, anyway.

Now, stroke the nail in the same direction 20 times with one pole of a bar magnet. Hold the nail to the paper clip again. Is the paper clip attracted? If so, the nail is now magnetic. You have created a magnet!

How did that work? By stroking the
nail over and over with one magnetic
pole, you attracted the magnetic domains
in the nail. Slowly, the north poles of all
the domains moved to face the same
way, so all the domains neatly lined up.

Because the nail's domains are lined up, the nail will now continue to be a magnet. The domains will stay lined up. Scientists call this a permanent magnet.

But even a permanent magnet can lose its magnetic force. If you hit a magnet several times with a hammer, the magnet will begin to lose its magnetism. This is because the physical force of the hammer breaks up the tiny domains and moves them in different directions. When the domains are no longer neatly lined up, the metal stops being a magnet.

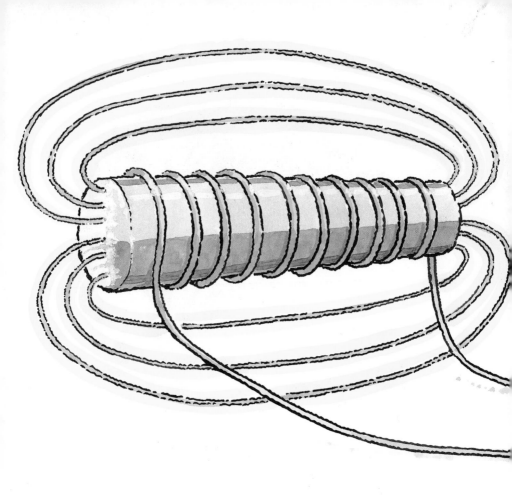

Another example of a nonpermanent
magnet is an electromagnet. Electromagnets
only stay magnetic for a short time.

When electricity flows through a wire,
it creates a magnetic field around the wire.
The more electricity there is, the stronger
the magnetic field. When wire is coiled

together, the electricity goes around and around a lot of times. There is a lot of electricity, so there's a strong magnetic field. Now the coil is a magnet.

When the electricity is turned off, the magnetic field goes away, and the coil is no longer a magnet.

Can you think of a way that a magnet that can be turned on and turned off might be a useful device?

When a car gets old or damaged, it usually ends up in a scrap yard. The car's steel is removed. It gets recycled and made into new things.

But how does a big, heavy car get lifted up and moved around? The steel in cars is attracted to magnets. You can lift a car with a strong electromagnet. Turn off the electromagnet. The car drops!

If the magnet could not be turned off, it would be hard to put the car back down again.

Magnet Earth

Do you know what the biggest magnet on our planet is? It <u>is</u> the planet! Planet Earth is a giant magnet, complete with a north pole, a south pole, and a magnetic field.

Deep inside, the earth's core is made up of solid iron and hot liquid iron. Remember: Iron is a very magnetic metal. The iron moves around as the earth rotates. This movement of iron creates a magnetic force.

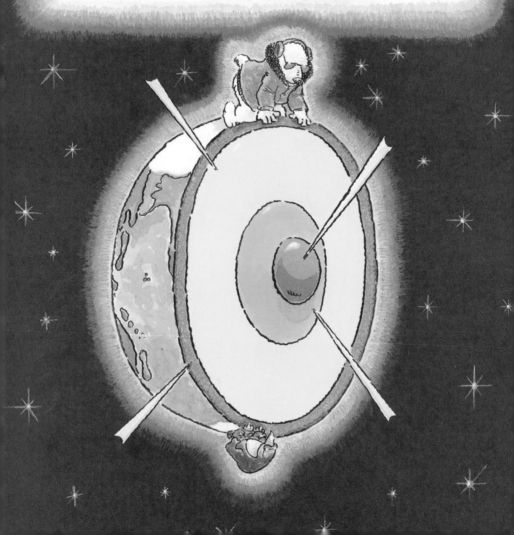

The earth's poles act like the poles of a giant magnet, attracting other magnetic objects to them.

For almost one thousand years, sailors have used the earth's magnetic field to find their way at sea. They use a tool called a compass. A compass is made of a magnetized needle that is attracted to the earth's north pole. So the compass needle always swings around to point north.

Like any magnet, the earth has a
magnetic field that wraps around it
from one pole to the other. Although
this field is usually invisible, you can
sometimes see it.

Some nights, far north or far south,

The northern and southern lights are an amazing light show in the sky.

particles get trapped in the earth's magnetic field. These particles create a pattern in the sky which is called aurora borealis (northern lights) in the north, and aurora australis (southern lights) in the south.

Compasses help people use the earth's magnetic force to find their way. Can animals use the earth's magnetic force as well?

Many animals migrate, or travel long distances, each year. How does a bird find its way from Canada to Mexico? How does a whale know which way to go when it is under water?

The earth's magnetic field may provide a magnetic map of the ocean for ahumpback whale to follow.

Are we there yet?

Monarch caterpillars get small amounts of magnetite from the milkweed flowers they eat.

Many animals (including humans!) have a small amount of magnetite in their brains. Scientists believe that some migratory animals use this magnetite to find north and south. They think this natural compass keeps the animals going in the right direction.

41

Magnets All Around

Our lives wouldn't be the same without magnets. Look around your house.

Do you have an electric can opener? It works by catching the top of the can with magnetic force. Does your refrigerator door stay closed? That's because the door is lined with a thin magnet.

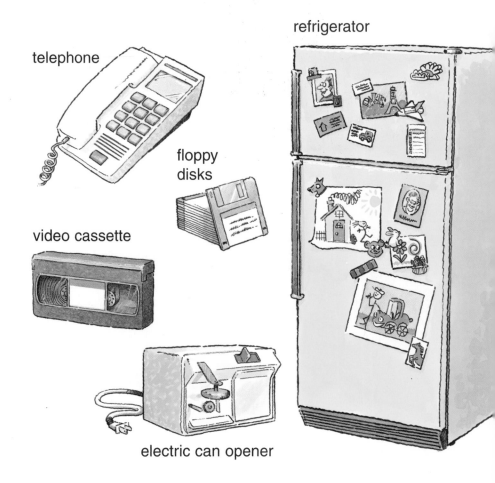

refrigerator

telephone

floppy disks

video cassette

electric can opener

Keep other magnets away from your computer. The magnetic force of another magnet can change the pattern of the information magnetically stored on your computer.

Do you ever use the computer? Special magnets inside help store information on floppy disks or on your hard drives. Have you ever spoken on the phone or watched a video? They wouldn't work without magnets either.

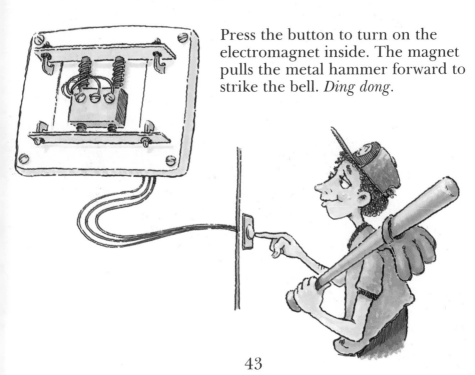

Press the button to turn on the electromagnet inside. The magnet pulls the metal hammer forward to strike the bell. *Ding dong*.

Step outside. Magnets are everywhere!
The force of magnetism can even stop
a train. A train's brakes use a powerful
magnetic field. Electromagnets in the
train's wheels are surrounded by other
electromagnets in the train's brakes.

When the train needs to brake, the electromagnets are turned on. As the wheel turns, it is first pushed and then pulled by the magnets in the brake. This makes the wheel slow down and then stop.

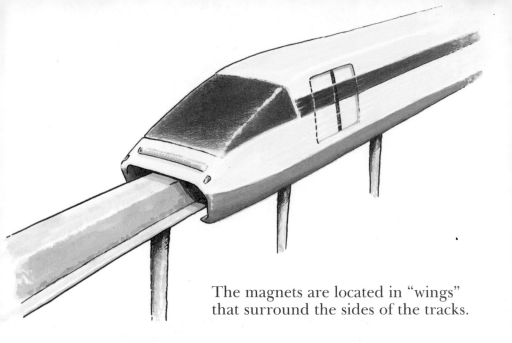

The magnets are located in "wings" that surround the sides of the tracks.

What is the future of magnet technology? There is already a highspeed train that floats above ground. The maglev train (named for magnetic levitation) uses the repelling force of magnets to move along a track. The train and track both contain magnets. The magnets' like poles face each other. These like poles repel each other and create a cushion of air between the train and the track. Floating above the air produces less friction. The train is fast and quiet.

One day, magnets might be used to launch a rocket into space. The idea is to put a satellite into a giant magnetic tube.

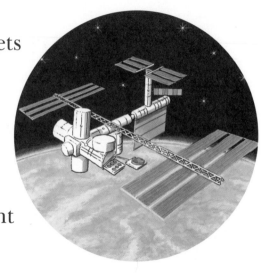

Electromagnetic rings would surround the tube. The electromagnets would pull the satellite up the tube, faster and faster, until it is shot out the end of the tube and into space.

Space exploration, transportation, energy production:—magnets might be used in so many ways. What new magnetic inventions can you think of?

GLOSSARY
The Meaning Is Magnetic

Attract: to pull toward

Domain: tiny magnetic regions inside a magnet

Electromagnet: a temporary magnet created by electricity and magnetism

Lodestone: a piece of magnetite

Magnes: ancient shepherd who discovered a magnetic rock.

Magnet: a material that has a magnetic force

Magnetic field: the area of magnetic force around a magnet

Magnetic poles: the areas of a magnet where the force is strongest

Magnetism: the force to attract or repel other objects

Magnetite: a rock made up of iron that acts as a natural magnet

Magnetosphere: the earth's magnetic field

Migration: traveling from one place to another each season

Nonpermanent magnet: a magnet in which the domains do not stay lined up over time

Northern lights: a display of the earth's magnetic field near the North Pole

Permanent magnet: a magnet in which the domains are lined up in one direction

Repel: to push away

Southern lights: a display of the earth's magnetic field near the South Pole